THE INDIAN ROYAL KITCHENS

A GASTRONOMIC JOURNEY THROUGH THE KITCHENS OF INDIA'S MAHARAJAS

DR. JAGADEESH PILLAI

Made with ♥ on the Notion Press Platform
www.notionpress.com

|| Dedicated to all wisdom seekers around the World ||

Contents

Contents

PRAYER

"Om Bhadram Karnebhih Shrunuyaama DevaahBhadram Pashyemaakshabhiryajatraah Sthirairangaistushtuvaamsastanoobhih Vyashema Devahitam YadaayuhSwasti Na Indro VridhashravaahSwasti Nah Pooshaa VishwavedaahSwasti Nastaarkshyo ArishtanemihSwasti No Brihaspatir DadhaatuOm Shantih, Shantih, Shantih"

The literal meaning of this mantra is: OM. O Gods! Let us hear auspicious words from our ears. O reverent Gods! Let us behold propitious visions from our eyes, let our organs and body be stable, healthy, and strong. Let us do that which is pleasing to the gods in the life span allotted to us. May Indra, inscribed in the scriptures, bring us fortune! May Pushan, the knower of the world, grant us prosperity! May Trakshya, who vanquishes enemies, bestow us with blessings! May Brihaspati bring us success!
OM Peace, Peace, Peace.

About The Author

Dr. Jagadeesh Pillai is a renowned Guinness World Record holder, writer, and researcher hailing from Varanasi, also known as the abode of Lord Shiva. With a Ph.D. in Vedic Science and a range of creative ideas and achievements, he is a true polymath. He is the author of more than 100 books including Research Publications. Although his roots can be traced back to Kerala, the people of Varanasi hold him in high regard and affectionately consider him one of their own.

In 1998, Dr. Pillai was offered a job at Banaras Hindu University, but he left the position after only two months to pursue greater goals in life. He believed that in order to study Indian scriptures and engage in other creative endeavours, he needed to retire from the daily grind of working solely for money at a young age.

He started an export business from scratch, using the knowledge he had gained from a previous job in the industry. His intelligence and unique approach to business led to great success in a short period of time, earning him more in just a decade and a half than he would have in a lifetime working in a government job. Upon the passing of Dr. APJ Abdul Kalam, Dr. Pillai decided to leave the business and dedicate himself to reading, studying, researching, and experimenting.

During his tenure in the export business, Dr. Pillai traveled to over 16 countries, gaining valuable insight and experiencing the world and life in detail.

Dr. Pillai has achieved four Guinness World Records in the following subjects:

"Script to Screen" - In this record, Dr. Pillai produced and directed an animation film within the shortest time possible, breaking the previous record set by Canadians. He has also received numerous national and international awards and recognitions for this achievement.

Longest Line of Postcards - For this record, Dr. Pillai created a line of 16,300 postcards on the occasion of the 163rd anniversary of Indian Postal Day. The event also included a questionnaire about the Indian flag.

Largest Poster Awareness Campaign - Dr. Pillai designed an awareness campaign on the subject of "Beti Bachao - Beti Padhao" (Save the Girl Child - Educate the Girl Child) to achieve this record.

Largest Envelope - In tribute to the Indian Prime Minister's "Make in India" initiative, Dr. Pillai created a 4000 square meter envelope using waste paper to achieve this record.

Attempted - **70000 Candles on a 210 kg Cake** - To celebrate the 70th Indian Independence Day, Dr. Pillai attempted to light 70,000 candles on a 210 kg cake, which was recorded in World Records India.

Attempted - **Documentary on Dhamek Stupa of Sarnath in 17 Languages** - Dr. Pillai attempted to create a documentary on the Dhamek Stupa of Sarnath, dubbing it in 17 different languages. The result of this attempt is currently awaiting confirmation from the Guinness World Records.

Dr. Pillai is skilled in teaching the Bhagavad Gita, a Hindu scripture, and is popular among young people. He has helped many young people improve their lives through his motivational teachings.

In addition to teaching, he has composed and sung numerous Sanskrit Bhajans and patriotic songs.

He has also written and directed several short films and documentaries for awareness campaigns, and has volunteered with the police in both UP and Kerala to spread awareness about various issues through videos and photography.

Incredibly, he has produced and directed over 100 documentaries about the city of Varanasi, all on his own.

He has also helped and guided more than 25 boys and girls to achieve world records through creative and innovative methods. He is a multifaceted person who uses his intellect and the blessings given to him by God to excel in various areas. He is both a teacher and a student, always learning and teaching, and is able to master any subject he comes across.

He is a selfless social activist and motivational speaker who has overcome struggles and failures to become a successful and enthusiastic individual with a rich life experience.

In addition to his work with the Bhagavad Gita, he is also an efficient Tarot card reader, Astro-Vastu consultant, and a talented singer and composer. He has sung the entire Ram Charita Manas and Bhagavad Gita in his own compositions, and has sung the phrase "Lokah Samastha Sukhino Bhavantu" in 50 different languages. He is currently working on a detailed and scientific study of Vedas, Upanishads, Puranas, and the Bhagavad Gita. He has also composed and sung the Hanuman Chalisa and Gayatri Mantra in 108 and 1008 different compositions, respectively.

Awards - Four Times Guinness World Records, Winner of Mahatma Gandhi Vishwa Shanti Puraskar, Mahatma Gandhi Global Peace Ambassador, Kashi Ratna Award, Dr. APJ Abdul Kalam Motivational Person of the Year 2017, Mother Teresa Award, Indira Gandhi Priyadarshini Award, Bharat Vikas Ratna Award, Udyog Ratna Award, Vigyan Prasar Award, Poorvanchal Ratn Samman.

PREFACE

The royal kitchens of India have been producing exquisite dishes for centuries. These kitchens have over time produced several iconic dishes that have been handed down through generations, creating a unique and varied gastronomic heritage. This book, The Indian Royal Kitchens: A Gastronomic Journey Through the Kitchens of India's Maharajas, seeks to explore the culinary traditions and secrets of the royal kitchens of India.

This book is intended to serve as an introduction to the rich history and culture of the Indian royal kitchens for readers who are new to the subject. It explores the various royal kitchens of India and their culinary traditions, techniques, and ingredients. It also examines the experiments in the royal kitchens, the rise in interest in royal cuisines, and the future of the Indian royal kitchens.

The book draws on research from a variety of sources, including interviews with key figures in the Indian royal kitchens industry, archival materials, and cultural analysis. I have also conducted extensive field research in India, including attending royal kitchen festivals, interviewing royal chefs, and visiting locations associated with the production of royal cuisines. Through this research, I hope to provide readers with a comprehensive understanding of the Indian royal kitchens industry and its various components.

I am deeply passionate about the art of the Indian royal kitchens and hope that this book will help to spread the appreciation of this wonderful form of cuisine. I believe that the Indian royal kitchens have a great deal to offer to the world and I am excited to share their cultural and historical significance with my readers.

A Indian Traditional Royal Kitchen

I

Introduction to the Indian Royal Kitchens

The Indian royal kitchens are renowned for their opulence and grandeur, reflecting the wealth and power of the country's Maharajas. These kitchens were the center of culinary excellence and were responsible for feeding royalty and their guests with an array of delectable dishes. From the lavish banquets of the Mughal courts to the sumptuous feasts of the Rajputs, the Indian royal kitchens offer a glimpse into the rich culinary heritage of India.

The Indian royal kitchens were known for their vast size, with many kitchens spanning thousands of square feet. They were equipped with multiple hearths and ovens, allowing for the preparation of an extensive menu of dishes. The kitchens employed a large staff, including chefs, bakers, and other culinary specialists, who were trained in the art of cooking and were responsible for creating the elaborate meals served in the royal courts.

The ingredients used in the Indian royal kitchens were of the highest quality, with spices and herbs imported from around the world. The kitchens also employed the use of exotic ingredients such as saffron, cinnamon, nutmeg, and clove, to create the rich and flavorful dishes that have become synonymous with Indian cuisine.

The culinary styles of the Indian royal kitchens were diverse, reflecting the different regions and cultural influences that shaped the country's cuisine. From the rich and spicy dishes of the Mughal courts to the lighter and fresher flavors of the coastal regions, the Indian royal kitchens offered a range of options to suit every taste.

One of the most distinctive features of the Indian royal kitchens was the use of traditional cooking methods, such as cooking over an open flame or in a tandoor oven. This not only imparted unique flavors to the dishes, but also allowed the chefs to prepare dishes that were impossible to make with modern cooking methods.

The Indian royal kitchens were also known for their elaborate presentations, with dishes often presented in elaborate silver platters and garnished with edible gold and silver. The banquets were a visual feast, with the dishes arranged in intricate patterns and decorated with colorful edible flowers and herbs.

The Indian royal kitchens offer a glimpse into the rich culinary heritage of India. From their vast size and grandeur, to the high-quality ingredients and traditional cooking methods, the Indian royal kitchens were a symbol of the wealth and power of the country's Maharajas. This book will take you on a gastronomic journey through the kitchens of India's Maharajas, showcasing the diversity and elegance of the country's culinary heritage.

"The Indian royal kitchens are a feast for the senses and a celebration of culinary tradition."

ꕤ

II

The Royal Kitchens of Rajasthan

Rajasthan, located in the northwestern region of India, is known for its rich cultural heritage and is home to some of the country's most famous royal kitchens. The kitchens of the Rajput rulers were renowned for their opulence and culinary prowess, and were the center of culinary excellence in the region. The dishes prepared in these kitchens reflect the unique blend of influences that have shaped the region's cuisine over the centuries, including Persian, Central Asian, and Mughal influences.

The Rajput rulers were known for their love of fine food and were known to host elaborate banquets in their palaces and forts. These banquets were attended by the elite of the kingdom, including nobles, scholars, and visiting dignitaries, and were renowned for their lavish spreads of rich and flavorful dishes. The kitchens were equipped with multiple hearths, ovens, and other cooking implements, and were staffed by a large team of skilled chefs and culinary specialists.

The ingredients used in the royal kitchens of Rajasthan were of the highest quality and were sourced from around the world. The region was known for its rich agriculture, and local ingredients such as ghee, milk, yogurt, and an array of spices and herbs were used in the preparation of dishes. The use of these ingredients, combined with traditional cooking methods such as slow cooking over an open flame, created dishes that were rich in flavor and aroma.

One of the most distinctive features of the royal kitchens of Rajasthan was their use of the tandoor oven. The tandoor is a clay oven that is heated to high temperatures, and is used to cook dishes such as naan bread, tandoori chicken, and kebabs. The intense heat of the tandoor imparts a unique smoky flavor to the dishes, which is sought after by food lovers around the world.

The dishes prepared in the royal kitchens of Rajasthan were known for their rich and complex flavors, and often featured bold combinations of spices and herbs. Some of the most famous dishes of the region include dal baati, a dish made of lentils and wheat balls that are slow cooked and then roasted in the tandoor; laal maas, a fiery red curry made with lamb and a blend of spices; and gatte ki sabzi, a dish made of chickpea flour dumplings in a spicy tomato and yogurt sauce.

The banquets in the royal kitchens of Rajasthan were known for their elaborate presentations, with dishes served on silver platters and garnished with edible gold and silver. The banquets were a feast for the senses, with the dishes arranged in intricate patterns and decorated with colorful edible flowers and herbs.

The royal kitchens of Rajasthan offer a glimpse into the rich culinary heritage of the region. From the use of traditional cooking methods, such as the tandoor oven, to the bold and complex flavors of the dishes, the royal kitchens of Rajasthan were a symbol of the wealth and power of the Rajput rulers. This book will take you on a gastronomic journey through the royal kitchens of Rajasthan, showcasing the unique blend of influences that have shaped the region's cuisine over the centuries.

"The heritage of the Indian royal kitchens is a precious treasure that must be preserved for future generations."

ꕤ

III

The Royal Kitchens of Awadh

Awadh, located in the northern region of India, was once the center of the rich and powerful kingdom of the same name. The kitchens of the Awadh royalty were renowned for their culinary prowess, and the dishes prepared in these kitchens have become some of the most famous and beloved in Indian cuisine. The Awadh cuisine is known for its use of fragrant spices and aromatic ingredients, and the dishes are characterized by their rich and decadent flavors.

The Awadh royalty were passionate about food, and the kitchens in their palaces and forts were staffed by a large team of skilled chefs and culinary specialists. The ingredients used in these kitchens were of the highest quality and were sourced from around the world. This included exotic spices and herbs, as well as ingredients such as saffron, almonds, and pistachios.

The dishes prepared in the Awadh kitchens were known for their elaborate presentations, with dishes arranged in intricate patterns and garnished with edible gold and silver. The banquets hosted by the Awadh royalty were famous for their opulence, and the rich and flavorful dishes were served on silver platters and accompanied by fine wines and other beverages.

The Awadh cuisine is characterized by its use of fragrant spices, including cardamom, cinnamon, clove, and nutmeg. These spices, combined with the use of aromatic ingredients such as saffron, kewra water, and rose petals, result in dishes that are rich in flavor and aroma. Some of the most famous dishes of the Awadh cuisine include biryani, a dish of basmati rice cooked with spices, meat, and vegetables; kebabs, succulent pieces of meat or vegetables that are marinated and grilled or roasted; and korma, a creamy and flavorful dish made with yogurt and spices.

The Awadh cuisine is also known for its use of slow cooking methods, such as the dum pukht technique. In this method, dishes are cooked over a low flame with a sealed lid, allowing the flavors to develop and intensify over time. This technique results in dishes that are rich, tender, and flavorful.

The royal kitchens of Awadh offer a glimpse into the rich and diverse cuisine of northern India. From the use of fragrant spices and aromatic ingredients, to the elaborate presentations of the dishes, the royal kitchens of Awadh were a symbol of the wealth and power of the kingdom. This book will take you on a gastronomic journey through the royal kitchens of Awadh, showcasing the unique blend of flavors and ingredients that have shaped the region's cuisine over the centuries.

"The grandeur and opulence of the Indian royal kitchens are unmatched, reflecting the grandeur of India's royalty."

ꙮ

IV

The Royal Kitchens of Patiala

Patiala, located in the northern state of Punjab, was once the capital of the powerful Patiala State. The kitchens of the Patiala royalty were renowned for their culinary skills, and the dishes prepared in these kitchens have become some of the most beloved in Punjabi cuisine. The Patiala cuisine is characterized by its rich and robust flavors, and the use of ingredients such as ghee, butter, and cream.

The kitchens in the Patiala palaces were staffed by a large team of skilled chefs and culinary specialists. These kitchens were equipped with the latest equipment and technology, and the ingredients used were of the highest quality. This included exotic spices, fresh herbs, and ingredients such as saffron, almonds, and pistachios.

The Patiala cuisine is characterized by its use of rich and creamy ingredients, such as ghee, butter, and cream. These ingredients, combined with fragrant spices such as cardamom, cinnamon, clove, and nutmeg, result in dishes that are rich and flavorful. Some of the most famous dishes of the Patiala cuisine include butter chicken, a rich and creamy dish made with tender chicken pieces in a spiced tomato-based sauce; tandoori chicken, a dish of marinated chicken that is grilled or roasted in a clay oven; and makki di roti, a flatbread made with maize flour and served with a side of spiced butter.

The Patiala cuisine is also known for its use of slow cooking methods, such as the dum technique. In this method, dishes are cooked over a low flame with a sealed lid, allowing the flavors to develop and intensify over time. This technique results in dishes that are rich, tender, and flavorful.

The royal kitchens of Patiala offer a glimpse into the rich and diverse cuisine of northern India. From the use of rich and creamy ingredients, to the elaborate presentations of the dishes, the royal kitchens of Patiala were a symbol of the wealth and power of the kingdom. This book will take you on a gastronomic journey through the royal kitchens of Patiala, showcasing the unique blend of flavors and ingredients that have shaped the region's cuisine over the centuries.

"The fusion of old and new in the Indian royal kitchens creates a harmonious balance of tradition and innovation."

A Indian Traditional Royal Kitchen

V

The Royal Kitchens of Bahawalpur

The kingdom of Bahawalpur, located in the northern region of present-day Pakistan, was known for its rich cultural heritage and lavish royal lifestyle. The royal kitchens of Bahawalpur were renowned for their intricate and flavorful dishes, and the use of fresh, locally-sourced ingredients.

The kitchens in the Bahawalpur palaces were staffed by a team of highly skilled and experienced chefs. These chefs were trained in the art of preparing dishes that were not only delicious, but also visually appealing. They used a variety of cooking techniques, such as baking, grilling, and roasting, to create dishes that were both delicious and nutritious.

One of the defining characteristics of the Bahawalpur cuisine is the use of spices and herbs. The region is known for its rich and fertile soil, which allowed for the growth of a variety of aromatic spices, such as cumin, coriander, and turmeric. These spices were used in a wide range of dishes, from rich and hearty stews to delicate, flavorful biryanis.

Another key aspect of the Bahawalpur cuisine is the use of locally-sourced ingredients. The region is known for its fertile land, and its cuisine reflects this abundance. Fresh fruits and vegetables, such as tomatoes, onions, and okra, were used in a variety of dishes, adding flavor and nutrition to the meals. Meat dishes, such as kebabs and tikkas, were also popular, and were made with high-quality cuts of meat, such as lamb and chicken.

The Bahawalpur cuisine is also known for its use of slow-cooking methods, such as the dum technique. In this method, dishes are cooked over low heat, with a sealed lid, allowing the flavors to develop and intensify over time. This technique results in dishes that are rich, tender, and flavorful.

The royal kitchens of Bahawalpur were renowned for their intricate and flavorful dishes, and their use of fresh, locally-sourced ingredients. The use of spices and herbs, combined with slow-cooking methods, has helped to create a cuisine that is both delicious and nutritious. This book will take you on a journey through the royal kitchens of Bahawalpur, showcasing the unique blend of flavors and ingredients that have shaped this region's cuisine over the centuries.

"The Indian royal kitchens are a testament to the richness of Indian cuisine and the skill of its chefs."

ஐ

VI

The Royal Kitchens of Gondal

The state of Gondal, located in the western region of present-day India, was known for its rich cultural heritage and lavish royal lifestyle. The royal kitchens of Gondal were renowned for their intricate and flavorful dishes, and the use of fresh, locally-sourced ingredients.

The kitchens in the Gondal palaces were staffed by a team of highly skilled and experienced chefs. These chefs were trained in the art of preparing dishes that were not only delicious, but also visually appealing. They used a variety of cooking techniques, such as baking, grilling, and roasting, to create dishes that were both delicious and nutritious.

One of the defining characteristics of the Gondal cuisine is the use of spices and herbs. The region is known for its rich and fertile soil, which allowed for the growth of a variety of aromatic spices, such as cumin, coriander, and turmeric.

These spices were used in a wide range of dishes, from rich and hearty stews to delicate, flavorful biryanis.

Another key aspect of the Gondal cuisine is the use of locally-sourced ingredients. The region is known for its fertile land, and its cuisine reflects this abundance. Fresh fruits and vegetables, such as tomatoes, onions, and okra, were used in a variety of dishes, adding flavor and nutrition to the meals. Meat dishes, such as kebabs and tikkas, were also popular, and were made with high-quality cuts of meat, such as lamb and chicken.

The Gondal cuisine is also known for its use of slow-cooking methods, such as the dum technique. In this method, dishes are cooked over low heat, with a sealed lid, allowing the flavors to develop and intensify over time. This technique results in dishes that are rich, tender, and flavorful.

The royal kitchens of Gondal were renowned for their intricate and flavorful dishes, and their use of fresh, locally-sourced ingredients. The use of spices and herbs, combined with slow-cooking methods, has helped to create a cuisine that is both delicious and nutritious. This book will take you on a journey through the royal kitchens of Gondal, showcasing the unique blend of flavors and ingredients that have shaped this region's cuisine over the centuries.

"The recipes of the Indian royal kitchens are a window into the cultural heritage of India."

༄

VII

The Royal Kitchens of Sailana

Sailana, a small princely state in the western region of India, was known for its rich cultural heritage and luxurious lifestyle. The royal kitchens of Sailana were renowned for their intricate and flavorful dishes, which were prepared using traditional cooking techniques and locally-sourced ingredients.

The kitchens in the Sailana palaces were staffed by a team of highly skilled and experienced chefs. These chefs were trained in the art of preparing dishes that were not only delicious, but also visually appealing. They used a variety of cooking techniques, such as baking, grilling, and roasting, to create dishes that were both delicious and nutritious.

One of the defining characteristics of the Sailana cuisine is the use of spices and herbs. The region is known for its fertile soil, which allowed for the growth of a variety of aromatic spices, such as cumin, coriander, and turmeric. These spices were used in a wide range of dishes, from rich and hearty stews to delicate, flavorful biryanis.

Another key aspect of the Sailana cuisine is the use of locally-sourced ingredients. The region is known for its fertile land, and its cuisine reflects this abundance. Fresh fruits and vegetables, such as tomatoes, onions, and okra, were used in a variety of dishes, adding flavor and nutrition to the meals. Meat dishes, such as kebabs and tikkas, were also popular, and were made with high-quality cuts of meat, such as lamb and chicken.

The Sailana cuisine is also known for its use of slow-cooking methods, such as the dum technique. In this method, dishes are cooked over low heat, with a sealed lid, allowing the flavors to develop and intensify over time. This technique results in dishes that are rich, tender, and flavorful.

The royal kitchens of Sailana were renowned for their intricate and flavorful dishes, and their use of fresh, locally-sourced ingredients. The use of spices and herbs, combined with slow-cooking methods, has helped to create a cuisine that is both delicious and nutritious. This book will take you on a journey through the royal kitchens of Sailana, showcasing the unique blend of flavors and ingredients that have shaped this region's cuisine over the centuries.

"The dishes of the Indian royal kitchens are a feast for the eyes as well as the palate."

☙

VIII

The Mughlai Cuisine

The Mughlai cuisine is a style of cooking that originated in the courts of the Mughal Empire in northern India. This cuisine is characterized by its rich and flavorful dishes, which are prepared using traditional cooking techniques, as well as a blend of spices and herbs.

The Mughal Empire was a melting pot of cultures and cuisines, and this is reflected in the diverse and flavorful dishes of the Mughlai cuisine. The cuisine was heavily influenced by Persian, Turkish, and Central Asian cooking styles, and the use of spices, such as saffron, cardamom, and cinnamon, helped to create dishes that were both fragrant and flavorful.

The Mughal kitchen was staffed by a team of highly skilled and experienced chefs, who used a variety of cooking techniques, such as roasting, grilling, and baking, to create dishes that were both delicious and visually appealing. Meat dishes were a staple of the Mughlai cuisine, and high-quality cuts of meat, such as lamb, chicken, and beef, were used in a variety of dishes, including kebabs, tikkas, and biryanis.

The Mughal cuisine is also known for its use of slow-cooking methods, such as the dum technique, which results in dishes that are tender, juicy, and full of flavor. This technique involves sealing the lid of a cooking pot and cooking the dish over low heat, allowing the flavors to develop and intensify over time.

Another defining aspect of the Mughal cuisine is the use of rich and creamy sauces and gravies, which help to balance the spices and flavors in the dishes. The use of cream, ghee, and yogurt in dishes, such as kormas and rogan josh, helps to create a rich and indulgent flavor that is both satisfying and delicious.

The Mughlai cuisine is a rich and flavorful style of cooking that originated in the courts of the Mughal Empire in northern India. The cuisine is characterized by its blend of spices and herbs, slow-cooking methods, and the use of rich and creamy sauces and gravies. This book will take you on a journey through the Mughlai cuisine, showcasing the unique blend of flavors and ingredients that have shaped this style of cooking over the centuries.

"The Indian royal kitchens have a unique blend of spices and flavors that are both complex and delicious."

༻

IX

Ingredients and Techniques of the Indian Royal Kitchens

The Indian Royal Kitchens were renowned for their intricate and flavorful dishes, which were created using a range of ingredients and cooking techniques that have been passed down through generations. The use of these ingredients and techniques helped to create dishes that were both delicious and visually appealing, and that reflected the wealth and prestige of the Indian royalty.

Ingredients:

Spices: Spices have always been an essential part of Indian cuisine, and the Royal Kitchens were no exception. A wide range of spices, such as turmeric, cumin, coriander, cardamom, and cinnamon, were used to create dishes that were both fragrant and flavorful.

Herbs: Herbs, such as mint, coriander, and curry leaves, were used to add freshness and flavor to dishes.

Meat: Meat dishes were a staple of the Royal Kitchens, and high-quality cuts of meat, such as lamb, chicken, and beef, were used in a variety of dishes, including kebabs, tikkas, and biryanis.

Dairy products: Dairy products, such as cream, ghee, and yogurt, were used to create rich and creamy sauces and gravies, which helped to balance the spices and flavors in the dishes.

Rice: Rice was a staple food in the Royal Kitchens, and it was used to create dishes such as biryanis and pulaos, which were often served as a main course.

Cooking Techniques:

Slow Cooking: Slow cooking techniques, such as the dum technique, were used to create dishes that were tender, juicy, and full of flavor. This technique involved sealing the lid of a cooking pot and cooking the dish over low heat, allowing the flavors to develop and intensify over time.

Grilling and Roasting: Grilling and roasting techniques were used to cook meat dishes, such as kebabs and tikkas, to perfection. These techniques helped to caramelize the surface of the meat, creating a crispy exterior and a juicy and flavorful interior.

Baking: Baking techniques were used to create dishes such as kulchas and naans, which were often served as a side dish.

Marination: Marination was an essential technique used in the Royal Kitchens, and it involved marinating meat, poultry, and fish in a mixture of spices, herbs, and yogurt, to help tenderize the meat and infuse it with flavor.

The Indian Royal Kitchens were renowned for their intricate and flavorful dishes, which were created using a range of ingredients and cooking techniques. The use of spices, herbs, dairy products, meat, and rice, combined with techniques such as slow cooking, grilling and roasting, baking, and marination, helped to create dishes that were both delicious and visually appealing, and that reflected the wealth and prestige of the Indian royalty. This book will explore these ingredients and techniques in more detail, showcasing the unique blend of flavors and ingredients that have shaped the cuisine of the Indian Royal Kitchens over the centuries.

"The Indian royal kitchens are a celebration of the country's history, culture, and culinary traditions."

ꟹ

X

Experiments in the Indian Royal Kitchens

The Indian royal kitchens were not just known for their rich and elaborate cuisine, but also for their innovative experiments in food and cooking. The royal chefs were constantly striving to come up with new recipes and cooking methods, to create dishes that were not only delicious but also visually stunning. These experiments in the royal kitchens resulted in some of the most iconic and beloved dishes of Indian cuisine.

One such experiment was the use of saffron and gold leaf. Saffron was used to add a rich and fragrant aroma to dishes, and the gold leaf was used to add a touch of luxury and elegance. For example, in the royal kitchens of Awadh, dishes such as the "shahi tukda", a bread pudding topped with saffron and gold leaf, became famous. The use of saffron and gold leaf also became a symbol of wealth and prosperity, and was a popular ingredient in many other dishes in the Indian royal kitchens.

Another experiment was the use of spices, which was a hallmark of the Indian royal kitchens. The royal chefs used a variety of spices in their dishes, such as cardamom, cinnamon, clove, nutmeg, and black pepper. They also experimented with different blends of spices, to create unique and complex flavors. For example, the “garam masala”, a blend of warm spices, became a staple ingredient in many of the dishes in the Indian royal kitchens.

The royal kitchens also experimented with cooking methods, such as slow cooking and roasting. Slow cooking was used to infuse the flavors of spices and herbs into the dishes, creating a rich and aromatic taste. Roasting was used to enhance the natural flavors of ingredients, such as meat and poultry, and to add a smoky and caramelized flavor to dishes. For example, the “biryani”, a dish made of rice, meat, and spices, was slow cooked over low heat, resulting in a delicious and fragrant dish.

In addition to these experiments, the Indian royal kitchens also introduced new ingredients to the cuisine, such as exotic fruits and vegetables, and exotic meats, such as venison and quail. The chefs in the royal kitchens were also known for their use of herbs, such as mint and coriander, to add freshness and flavor to their dishes.

The experiments in the Indian royal kitchens were not just limited to the creation of new dishes and cooking methods, but also included the use of new cooking utensils and equipment. The royal kitchens were equipped with the latest cooking equipment, such as tandoors, clay ovens, and kadhai pans, which allowed the chefs to cook dishes with precision and control.

The experiments in the Indian royal kitchens were a major contributor to the rich and diverse cuisine that is loved and enjoyed today. These experiments, which combined traditional cooking methods with innovative techniques, resulted in the creation of dishes that are not only delicious, but also visually stunning, and have become a hallmark of Indian cuisine.

"The Indian royal kitchens have set the standard for grand feasts and elaborate dining experiences."

༄

XI

The Future of the Indian Royal Kitchens

Introduction:

The Indian royal kitchens have a rich and fascinating history dating back centuries. These kitchens once held the epitome of culinary excellence and set the standard for grand and elaborate feasts. Despite the decline of royalty in India, the traditions and techniques of the royal kitchens continue to live on today. This chapter will explore the future of these kitchens, the impact they have on Indian cuisine, and the ways in which they are adapting to modern times.

Preserving the Traditions:

The Indian royal kitchens have a wealth of knowledge and

skills that have been passed down through generations of cooks. This is a treasure trove of cultural heritage that must be preserved for future generations. Today, the descendants of the royal families and the chefs who once worked in their kitchens are working to keep the traditions alive. Cooking classes and food festivals are being organized to showcase the unique dishes and techniques of the Indian royal kitchens. This helps to raise awareness and appreciation for these kitchens and their contributions to Indian cuisine.

Incorporating Modern Techniques:

While preserving the traditions is important, the Indian royal kitchens are also adapting to modern times. With the increasing popularity of Indian cuisine worldwide, the kitchens are experimenting with new techniques and ingredients to stay ahead of the curve. They are also exploring ways to make traditional dishes healthier, such as reducing the amount of oil and sugar used in recipes. This helps to bring the Indian royal kitchens into the modern era while still maintaining their signature flavor and style.

Collaborations with Chefs and Restaurants:

Another way the Indian royal kitchens are adapting to modern times is through collaborations with chefs and restaurants. These partnerships allow for the sharing of knowledge and expertise between the traditional royal kitchens and modern culinary institutions. This can lead to the creation of new dishes and new interpretations of traditional recipes. The result is a fusion of old and new, which is both exciting and delicious.

The Indian royal kitchens have a rich history and a bright future. They are adapting to modern times while still preserving their traditions and techniques. The impact they have on Indian cuisine is significant and will continue to be felt for generations to come. The future of the Indian royal kitchens is filled with exciting possibilities, and it will be fascinating to see how they continue to evolve and grow. Whether it's through cooking classes, food festivals, collaborations with chefs, or the incorporation of modern techniques, the Indian royal kitchens are poised for continued success in the future.

A Indian Traditional Royal Kitchen Hall

"The intricate and elaborate dishes of the Indian royal kitchens are a work of art and a gastronomic masterpiece."

"The techniques and recipes of the Indian royal kitchens are a testament to the mastery of its chefs."

"The Indian royal kitchens are a culinary journey that takes the taste buds on a trip through India's rich history and culture."

"The future of the Indian royal kitchens is filled with exciting possibilities, as they continue to evolve and grow."

"The Indian royal kitchens are a gastronomic treasure that will continue to inspire and delight food lovers for generations to come."

&

Other Books Of The Author

1. The Moments When I Met God
2. Kashiyile Theertha Pathangal
3. GURU GYAN VANI
4. Abhiprerak Gita
5. ASSI SE JAIN GHAT TAK
6. Hopelessness of Arjuna
7. The Soul and It's True Nature
8. Sense of Action (Karma)
9. Action through Wisdom
10. Action through Wisdom
11. THEORY AND PRACTICAL OF EVERY ACTION
12. LOGICAL UNDERSTANDING OF THE SUPREME
13. THE IMPERISHABLE SUPREME
14. Yatra Nishadraj se Hanuman Ghat Tak
15. Yatra Karnatak Ghat se Raja Ghat Tak
16. Yatra Pandey Ghat se Prayagraj Ghat Tak
17. Yatra Ranjendra Prasad Ghat se Dattatreya Ghat Tak
18. YaatraSindhiya Ghat se Gwaliar Ghat Tak
19. Yatra Mangala Gauri Ghat se Hanuman Gadhi Ghat Tak
20. Yatra Gaay Ghat Se Nishad Ghat Tak
21. MAA GANGA, GHATEN EVM UTSAV
22. Ganga Arti Dev Deepavali evam Any Utsav
23. Potentials of Digitalized India
24. VEDIC CONSCIOUSNESS
25. A Brief Introduction to Vedic Science
26. Kashi ke Barah Jyotirling
27. IMPACT OF MOTIVATION
28. Let's have a Milky Way Journey
29. Color Therapy in a Nutshell

30. Rigveda in a Nutshell
31. Yajurveda in a Nutshell
32. Samveda in a Nutshell
33. Atharva Veda in a Nutshell
34. Ayushman Bhava - Ayurveda
35. Srimad Bhagavad Gita and Upanishad Connection
36. Srimad Bhagavad Gita - an attempt to summarize each chapter.
37. Facts and Impact of Nakshatra
38. Astro Gems - NAVARATNA
39. Ekadashi - A Concise Overview
40. A Concise View of Hanuman Chalisa
41. Inspirational Gita
42. Nakshatraranyam
43. Summary of 18 Mahapuranas
44. Synopsis of 18 Upa Puranas
45. Rigvediya Upanishads
46. Shukla Yajurvediya Upanishads
47. Krishna Yajurvediya Upanishads
48. Samavediya Upanishads
49. Atharvavediya Upanishads
50. The Seven Great Sages
51. From Rocket Scientist to President Dr. APJ Abdul Kalam
52. The Visionary's Voice - Quotes of Dr. APJ Abdul Kalam
53. The Wisdom of Swami Vivekananda: Insights and Inspiration from a Legendary Spiritual Teacher
54. Ayurvedic Remedies from the Garden
55. Sages and Seers
56. Rising Strong – Motivational Stories of Women
57. Beyond Flames -Mystery stories of Funeral Ghat Manikarnika
58. The Origins of Tulsi: A Look at the Mythological Roots of the Plant"

59. The Holistic Cow: A Look at the Physical, Spiritual, and Cultural Importance of Cows in India
60. Arts of Healing
61. Exploring the Divine
62. Understanding Five Elements
63. The Etymology of Ram
64. Symbols of India
65. Voice of Change (About Speeches of Great Men)
66. She Speaks (About Speeches of Great Women)
67. Patriotism on Celluloid – Brief About Patriotic Films
68. The Music of Motivation: A Brief Guide to Inspirational Film Songs
69. **Unlocking the Secrets of the Dashopanishads**
70. A Cultural Mosaic
71. Ancient Traditions, Modern Minds
72. Ecos of Ancient Wisdom
73. Beneath the Surface
74. From Temples to Ashrams
75. Sages of the Subcontinent
76. The Art of Healling (Ayurveda, Yoga & Naturopathy)
77. Indian Kitchen
78. The Festivals of India
79. The Indian Epics Retold
80. The Power of Mantras
81. The Indian River Ganges
82. The Indian Architecture
83. Rites of Passage
84. The Indian Silk Road
85. The Indian Literature
86. The Indian Villages
87. The Indian Folks & Crafts
88. The Way of Buddha
89. The Ramayan of Tulsidas

90. Astrological Remedies
91. The Secret Power of Motivation
92. Secret of Developing your Inner Strength
93. The Secret Path to Motivation
94. The Art and Secret of Positive Thinking
95. The Secrets of Practicing Ethical Living
96. Indian Art and Painting
97. The Indian Herbalism
98. Bharatanatyam to Kathak
99. Exploring India's Astrological Remedies
100. The Indian Festival of Flowers
101. Indian Handicrafts
102. The Splashes of Joy – India's Colour Festival
103. The Indian Science of Astrology
104. The Indian Mythology
105. Path to Enlightenment
106. The Indian Spirituality for Children
107. Aromas of India
108. The Secrets of Healthy Relationships
109. Ancestral Ties
110. The Indian Street Food
111. Discovering America
112. The Indian Textile
113. Listening to Motivational Speeches
114. Taste of India
115. A Cultural Journey through Indian Nuptials
116. Motivational Quote for Change
117. Secret Strategies for Making Money
118. Secrets to Cultivate a Positive Mindset
119. A Tapestry of Cultures: Exploring India from Kashmir to Kanyakumari
120. Achieving Your Dreams with Resilience: Secret Strategies for Overcoming Obstacles

121. Innovative Startups - 25 Startup Ideas to Spark Your Business Creativity
122. Export Management: Strategies for Global Success
123. Exporting from India - A Step by Step Guide
124. Finance Fundamentals: Mastering Financial Management for Business Success
125. Global Growth Strategies for International Business Development
126. Marketing Mastery: Unlocking the Secrets of Modern Marketing
127. Operations Mastery: Managing the Flow of Value in Business
128. Strategic Business Management: Navigating the Modern Business Landscape
129. Human Resource Management Strategies for Building and Managing a High Performance Team
130. The Indian Landscapes and Nature: An Exploration Of India's Natural Beauty And Diversity
131. The Indian Street Performances: A Cultural Exploration of India's Street Performances
132. Affirming Your Self-Worth: Strategies for Achieving Emotional Wellbeing
133. Cultivating Self-Discipline: Secrets Methods for Achieving Your Goals
134. Embracing Change: Strategies for Adapting to Life's Challenges
135. Embracing Your Uniqueness: Secret Strategies for Living an Authentic Life
136. Finding Motivation in Despondency: Coping with Difficult Times
137. Embracing Change
138. Learning to Love Yourself
139. Managing Time for Yourself

140. Unlock the keys to Self-Motivation
141. Secret to Boost Confidence
142. Unlocking your Potential: A Path to Inner-strength & Success
143. Secrets to Develop Authentic Relationship
144. Secrets to Build a Successful Career
145. Secrets to Live with Gratitude
146. Secrets to Create a Life of Abundance
147. Secrets to Cultivate Self-Awareness
148. The Power of Helping Hands
149. Finding Your Passion
150. The Indian Mythical Creatures
151. The Indian Women Saints
152. The Wisdom of the Saints
153. "The Indian Royalty: A Cultural and Historical Exploration of India's Maharajas and their kingdom"
154. The Mystic Land: A Cultural and Spiritual Exploration of India"
155. India's Spiritual Legacy – Discovering the Cultural and Religious Significance of Bhakti Yoga.
156. The Indian Folktales: An Exploration of India's Oral Folklore Traditions
157. Steeping In History: A Look at India's Iconic Tea Culture
158. The Indian Way Of Life: An Exploration Of The Philosophy And Practices Of Indian Culture
159. From Silence to Sound: A Cultural and Historical Study of Indian Cinema
160. Chronicles of Indian Style: Tracing the Transformations of Traditional and Contemporary Fashion
161. Decorating India: A Journey Through the Traditions and Transformations of Home Design
162. Adornments of India: A Journey Through the History and Artistry Behind Indian Jewelry

163. The Indian Royal Kitchens: A Gastronomic Journey Through the Kitchens of India's Maharajas

Contact

DR. JAGADEESH PILLAI

MBA & PhD in Vedic Science

Four Times Guinness World Record Holder

Winner of Mahatma Gandhi Vishwa Shanti Puraskar and
Global Peace Ambassador

Gemology, Astro & Vastu Consultant - Spiritual Counselor

Consultant for designing World Record Ideas

Efficient Tarot Card Reader

9839093003

myrichindia@gmail.com

drjagadeeshpillai@facebook

drjagadeeshpillai@instagram
jagadeeshpillai@youtube

www. JAGADEESHPILLAI.com

|| LOKAHA SAMASTHAHA SUKHINO BHAVANTU ||

ഇ

9 798889 595656

Printed by Libri Plureos GmbH in Hamburg,
Germany